T0265569

QUIET CREEK PUBLISHING

FIREFLY!

A Book of Poetry

*Poems that will make you
think, laugh and cry.*

WRITTEN BY

JACQUELINE ANDREA LAVALLE

2024

PUBLISHED BY

QUIET CREEK PUBLISHING

A BOOK OF POETRY

Visit quietcreekpublishing.com

ISBN: 979-8-2620-1-6 (print)   979-8-9872620-3-0 (ePub)

Printed and bound in the United States of America

"Poetry is a form of expression"

"Writing poetry lets us release our feelings and thoughts while reading it encourages us to connect and find meaning in our experiences. Poetry can have a positive impact on the social and emotional learning of children. It may offer them a new way of thinking about something.

"Poetry is so important because it helps us understand and appreciate the world around us. Poetry's strength lies in its ability to shed a "sideways" light on the world, so the truth sneaks up on you. No question about it. Poetry teaches us how to live."

--Author Unknown

WHERE DO POEMS COME FROM?

Every poet in the world will have a different answer.

For me they originate from many different places.

An overheard conversation, an event, an observation or an experience. And what about the influence of other poets?

I have at least two favorite poets: Langston Hughes (1902-1967) and John Keats (1795-1821), both of whom have inspired me greatly.

One of Langston Hughes' poems inspired a playwright to name one of her plays after a line in his poem. The title is *A Raisin in the Sun,* by Lorraine Hansberry (also known as *A Dream Deferred*). Hughes' poem so catches the essence of her play that it's as if he wrote it to explain the play.

Another poem by Langston Hughes, an African-American, *The Negro Speaks of Rivers*, can be found etched in the Library floor of *The Schomburg Collection for Research in Black Culture*. This poem has been incorporated in a stunning work of art—as a peace memorial, in honor of the poet. It is a brass cosmogram located permanently in the *Schomburg Center's Langston Hughes* lobby. It elegantly and profoundly expresses how people of color have been part of history since ancient times.

John Keats (1795-1821), was a British poet who wrote a very beautiful and romantic poem, *Ode to a Nightingale*, In it Keats praises the song of a bird who sings so beautifully that his mind is transported into an other-worldly experience.

I could never write like these legendary poets but if it wasn't for poets like these, I believe poetry would not have survived; and had I not discovered them and many others I (and many other poets) would not have developed the desire to write poetry.

Recently, a former poet laureate of the United States, Tracy K. Smith, commented that "poetry can often call on something deep within us."

I hope that this collection of poems will do the same for whom-ever decides to read *Firefly*.

--Jacqueline Lavalle

CONTENTS

Acknowledgments 113

A Certain Religion 107

A Hug 75

All About Fireflies 110-112

A Lullabye 59

An Ant (For The Young At Heart) 21

An Ode To Two Unfinished Glasses Of Guiness 25

Asparagus (For The Young At Heart) 55

At IKEA With My Sister 49

Autumn 61

Barley And Beans (For The Young At Heart) 53

Carpetti From Lake Erie (For The Young At Heart) 15

Comin' Round The Bend (For Bettors Everywhere) 31

Dandelions 63

Drums On My Ceiling 94-95

El Bongosero 103

Einstein's Theory 65

CONTENTS

Firefly, Firefly..13

For People Who Insist On Being Practical......................105

I Did What I Had To Do..33

In The Main, There's Champagne....................................27

Introduction...5

I Regret...73

It's Hard...39

Librarians..51

Librarians Are Dj's..71

Library Rap...99

Lolly Pop (For The Young At Heart)..43

Night Shift In Cleveland....................... 28-29

Palm Trees...89

Park Avenue Mansion, Number 515..................................37

Paul Gauguin...105

Poetic Justice...107

Rosarita Beach...45

CONTENTS

Rosie's Cardinal--A Conversation In Milford 67

Song For Steelworkers 69

Summer 101

The Carousel Of Forgotten Dreams 23

The Cherrywood Desk 47

The Dancer Of Toa Baja 83

The Fly And The Broken Wheel Bar 78-79

The Girl From The Ronkonkoma Line 17

The Lemonade Kids 87

The Man-In-The-Moon 77

The Playground Legend 81

The Swing Shift 85

Try Your Luck At Saratoga Or Do You Know
  Where Your Horse Was Last Night? 108-109

Tyre Nichols 91

Watermelons (For The Young At Heart) 57

Watermelons II 97

CONTENTS

We Are The City..41

Where Do Poems Come From?.........................7

Who Are The Cave Dwellers? 35

Women Are Like Trees....................................19

"June 12, 1991"...93

"so brief their courtship flight"

FIREFLY, FIREFLY

· ·

How simple in love a firefly!
  So brief their courtship flight;
And so on us the eternal eye
  blinks and we're out of sight.

"he'd swim the lake to see me"

CARPETTI FROM LAKE ERIE

· ·

Carpetti was carp
    who lived in old Lake Erie;
And every summer night
    he'd swim the lake to see me.
One day while he was swimming,
    he found the ideal mate.
Now with love he's brimming,
    and doesn't need a date.

"and she's still on the trains."

THE GIRL FROM THE RONKONKOMA LINE

· ·

She emerged bleary-eyed and cold into
    Penn station—a
    gloomy oasis of fresh squeezed
Orange juice, Nedicks and Dashing Dan.
    The Big City and the girl from "the sticks",
on her way to Hunter College.
       Twenty years later, she has a job
       and she's still on the trains.
Homeless men and women beseech her
    for money;
she listens to musicians who appear
    out of nowhere and
       give relief to the endless waiting.
But it's what she always wanted
    and her father said she needed:
A station in life.

"birds fly into their branches"

WOMEN ARE LIKE TREES

· ·

Women are like trees.
>Men are like birds.
The birds fly into their branches
>and nest there.
>>Trees stay put—
>>they have many roots.
Birds fly from tree to tree.
>and the trees worry
about the baby birds,
>trying so hard to fly.

"*she's found in every yard*"

For The Young At Heart

AN ANT

. . . .

An ant is a creature
who works very hard
    and besides that feature,
    she's found in every yard.
She labors by the hours,
    with little time for play.
Thank heavens for the flowers
    that brighten up her day!

"the organ played an
enchanting tune"

THE CAROUSEL OF FORGOTTEN DREAMS

. . . .

I came upon a carousel
    like one I've rarely seen;
the kind that lets one's age creep back
    to Fantasy and dream.

The music played and the riders swayed,
    the ponies went up and down,
each one painted with colors so gay,
    on this wonderful merry-go-round.
I listened as the organ played an enchanting tune
    and my thoughts away were transported soon:
Those gentle hands that placed me there,
    high on a pony and smoothed my hair;

"I'll wave" I shouted, "you wave too!"
    (That was best of all I knew).
As the music played and the rider's swayed
    and the ponies went up and down;

Alas, I had forgotten the dreams that I dreamed
    on the wonderful merry-go-round!

"...Two men, two glasses"

AN ODE TO TWO UNFINISHED GLASSES OF GUINESS IN MULLIGAN'S PUB, DUBLIN, IRELAND.

. . . .

Two men,
     two glasses,
unfinished
     but not
diminished.

"a sip of those bubbles"

IN THE MAIN
THERE'S CHAMPAGNE

· ·

In the main there's champagne,
what a drink
And to think,
a sip of those bubbles
is a trip
from your troubles.

NIGHT SHIFT IN CLEVELAND

There's fire in the sky!
But don't call the firemen,
    it's only the steel mills–
    they never sleep.

From the highways, the mills
    are huge and quiet;
    long buildings painted black,
    brown and red;
    covered with iron dust and
    shrouded in dirty mist and fog.

But who is that solitary figure
    passing through the gate?
Last one in for the night shift—
    that one with
    his hard hat in hand and
    thermos under his arm—
    he'll have a time of it.

continued....☛

NIGHT SHIFT IN CLEVELAND

· ·

He'll roll steel sleepy-eyed
   when he should be rolling over
   in his bed. He'll climb 100 steps to a crane,
   while his head aches for a soft pillow.

 Amid the deafening roar and clash
   of metal and machine;
   amid choking graphite dust and acid fumes
   he will move before the morning sun…
   tons of steel.

"Heads up!" The warnings
   come through the night.

Sirens. Whistles. Bells. "Watch out!"

And as the steel goes rolling on
   he'll fight to stay awake and alive.

And in the quiet night, high above the mills,
   there's fire in the sky!

"lady luck will see them through"

COMIN' ROUND THE BEND — (FOR BETTORS EVERYWHERE)

· ·

The OTB† is where bliss is,
    even better than loving kisses;
even you, can be a winner,
    over at the OTB.
But winning isn't really the game;
    adrenaline is the proper name:
desperate souls—jumpy and lost,
    waiting for the finish no matter the cost.
Soon as spring comes they rush to the track,
    grab their last dollar and don't look back;
here there is no self or caring—
    just vacant thoughts and lots of staring.
No matter that the rent is due,
    lady luck will see them through.
And so the ponies go round and round,
    in endless circles on the dusty ground.
And bettors play their very last dollar,
    and no one even gives a holler;
owners have fun: they're oh so chummy,
    as they run to their Porches with (bettors) money.
But hear me players! Don't you fret!
    The betting game's not over yet;
the RUSH goes on and will never end,
    your favorite horse is comin' round the bend!

"I tried so hard to play in your backyard"

I DID WHAT I HAD TO DO

I did what I had to do
    to be loved by you;
that was the time,
    I thought it sublime.
Yes, to be oh—so wanted,
    so, I went on—undaunted.
I tried so hard,
    to play in your backyard;
    then I discovered you were no good,
so I moved out of the neighborhood.

"our worldly possessions in boxes"

WHO ARE THE CAVE DWELLERS?

· ·

We are the poor people
    who live in quarters so small,
we wonder if the sides of mountains
    would be better?
We move around our dwellings sideways,
    and our walls from floor to ceiling
are decorated with shelves
    (that jut out) where
we place our worldly possessions (in boxes)
    and hit our heads on them.
We are the cave dwellers.
    Not to be confused with those who live in
subways and under bridges and
    wish they could afford a cave.

"your wish, madam, is my command"

[This poem was inspired by the <u>New York Times</u> article on 4/25/98, p.1, A HAVEN FOR THE SUPER-RICH WITH ROOM FOR THE SERVANTS. *The article begins: "In a city of gargantuan ambition, where Wall Street Boom and soaring corporate profits have bestowed fabulous riches on a few, it was perhaps only a matter of time until someone came up with 515 Park Avenue."*

515 PARK AVENUE MANSION

You over there with your nose in the air,
>welcome to Park Avenue!

Here you live in splendor and style,
>you need only give orders and force a smile.

A servant will descend each valuable floor,
>and bring whatever to your polished door.

And when you're hungry and wish to dine
>the cook makes a meal—no less than divine.

You plan to go to the Charity Ball?
>Nothing to wear? No worries at all!

The buyer at Bendel's awaits your call;
>he'll choose a costume for short or tall.

But first to sink into a nice warm bath;
>YOU draw the water? Don't make me laugh!

The house maid does it with practiced hand,
>"Your wish, Madam, is my command!"

Now you leave your Park Avenue Mansion;
>the limousine waits—doormen at attention…

But what is this? No one in sight?
>Something's amiss…Why they're all on strike!

And there you stand so awfully dejected,
>your charity, so abruptly rejected.

"it's hard to get up and dress"

IT'S HARD

· ·

Some days it's hard to begin,
    it's hard to get up and dress;
you'd rather stay in––
    besides, your hair's a mess.

The hot water isn't working,
    you don't have a thing to wear.
You just don't feel like chirping,
    just nesting in your chair!

"we work 24 hours a day"

WE ARE THE CITY

We are the city.
>We are all colors, all ages, all religions,
>men and women.

We raise the skyscrapers and
>wash their windows.

Sometimes you see us dangling.

We lay pipe and cable underneath
>the City's streets.

Sometimes you see us
>climbing out of "man" holes.

We transport packages, letters
>and people.

And when all is said and done,
>we pick up what the City leaves behind—
>all the refuse of life and living.

Some of us are:
>Ill-fed; Ill-clothed; Ill-housed; Ill-paid,
>Ill.

And when we're injured or sick,
>we repair our bodies in hospitals
>where we work 24-hours a day;

So the City can keep on living,
>men and women.

All colors, all ages, all religions.
>We are the City.

"you bright and sassy candystick"

For The Young At Heart

LOLLIPOP

. . . .

Oh lolly, lolly, lolly pop;
    you're tried and true—
    the very top—
    you bright and sassy candystick,
you sweeten me with every lick!

"she wanders about the shore"

ROSARITA BEACH

. . . .

Fishermen only whisper her name,
    as she walks with
    the changing moon and
    gazes on the tide's dark secrets.

And like the shells upon the sand
that have lost their souls,
    she wanders about the shore
    with no place
    to rest her heart.

"a miraculous collection of notes"

THE CHERRYWOOD DESK

Of what have they writ on this Cherrywood Desk,
   for it is empty and its secrets gone?
A love letter penned by a shy suitor?
   and did he send it after all—
A note of thanks for a kindness rendered?
   (Kind deeds should always be so honored.)
A song?
   A miraculous collection of notes
   to woo a crowd or a lover;
a joyful announcement of a baby's Birth,
   and how it must have changed their lives!
And if they writ about a birth on this table
   surely they have writ about a death?
It comes even as a newborn comes.
   An array of checks to God knows who,
for God knows what;
   a surface to sign away a day's pay.
Have they writ letters to friends
   who have moved away,
out of one's life and into another?
And now through space and time
   the Cherrywood Desk
has come to you;
   guard it well, for it is heavy with life.

"it's the place for any idea"

AT IKEA WITH MY SISTER

YOU say you haven't been to IKEA?
It is the place for any idea!
So I went there with my sister;
I say, old chum, you couldn't miss her!
Her dark hair and blue eyes so charming,
she's quite disarming.
(Her eyes peeled…her demeanor steeled)
Her nose wiggled and pointed to the chase,
Her feet moved at a maddening pace;
Baskets and blankets and pots and pans;
towels and spoons and watering cans;
Tiles and tables, toys and rugs;
bowls and platters and coffee mugs.
Do they have elephants ? I can't be certain;
you can buy a chair or a shower curtain.
And if you get hungry, don't despair,
You can eat lingonberry and caviar!
You say you've never been to IKEA?
Let me give you a great idea..
go with my sister —she's a sight to behold:
like a miner with a dream in search of gold.

"we really do love our books"

LIBRARIANS

· ·

Men and women forever curious.
We really do have passion
    and are mostly people of action.
We don't wear our hair in a bun
    and frequently capable of a pun.
We do love our books;
    and sometimes are not bad for looks.
Our environment does get dusty…
    BUT SURELY WE ARE NEVER FUSTY!

"Mom and Dad put them on a plate"

For The Young At Heart

BARLEY AND BEANS

· ·

Barley and beans,
　　barley and beans,
Molly and Bret
　　love barley and beans.
Mom and Dad put them on a plate;
　　Molly and Bret ate and ate.
After Dad took away the dishes
　　Molly and Bret said "They were delicious!"
Barley and beans,
　　Barley and beans;
Bret and Molly
　　love Barley and beans!

"which part of them do you eat?"

For The Young At Heart

ASPARAGUS

. . . .

I'm not wild about asparagus,
Though they always look so neat.
And I wonder about artichokes,
which part of 'em do you eat?
Peas you can eat with ease
but they roll around your plate.
I'll take spinach over any of these
Cuz that's what Popeye ate!

"and slice into a smile"

For The Young At Heart

WATERMELONS

· ·

Watermelons are green and pink
and slice into a smile;
as I eat and lick my cheek,
summer lingers awhile!

"it's good to sleep and not ask why"

A LULLABYE

· ·

When light'ning strikes and thunder roars;
    when gray skies open and it rains and
    pours;
it's good to sleep and not ask why:
    the heavens sent a lullabye.

"as if her summer was well spent"

AUTUMN

· ·

I saw a leaf sail off a tree
    so happily, carelessly.
As if her summer was well spent
    without a hitch:
As if when she reached the ground
    she would sail up again—
Be green and see another summer.

"they dally by the side of the road"

DANDELIONS

· ·

Dandelions are dandy
　　because they're so handy;
Even as the little brown toad,
　　they dally by the side of the road!

"the universe...was made to order"

EINSTEIN'S THEORY

There is nothing we dread
    like an unmade bed;
Tolerate we can't
    an unwatered plant.
A room is supreme
    when after we clean;
Life could be sweeter
    if we were neater!
The universe—for rich or poorer—
    like this verse—was made to order.

"He should have a royal breakfast"

ROSIE'S CARDINAL—
A CONVERSATION IN MILFORD

· ·

"He was here a second ago."
    "Who? Oh you mean the Cardinal!"
"He darted by your doorway and
    then he was gone…I imagine
he thought there was a morsel here
    to tempt him."
"He should have a royal breakfast."
    "Oh yes! A fine prince with a
crimson mantle and black cap!"
    "That's royalty for you, they love to make
brief appearances."

"and so we built the USA"

SONG FOR STEELWORKERS

Oh the steel, the steel is rolling
    and the coils turning round
And there you see us working
    on the cranes and on the ground.
We're sweeping and we're hauling,
    got the foremen on our back
Got to keep the steel from spoiling.
    got to move it off the rack.
And the flatbeds keep on coming
    to haul the steel away.
And the drivers keep on trucking
    from Cleveland to L.A.
It's we who make the steel
    and we who run the cranes
    and we who run the box anneal;
    and we who rig the chains.
It's we who stoke the coke
    and we who turn the mold
    and we who set the steel to soak.
And we who haul it cold…
    and so we built the USA.
Its buildings, its highways and so much more.
Then one day they shut the door
    and took our pensions away and
    our sweat…our blood…our tears…
Our devoted labor and all our years.

"we spin ideas"

LIBRARIANS ARE DJ'S

· ·

Librarians are the DJ's of knowledge.
　　We don't spin records,
　　we spin ideas.
We scratch out the world
　　and its mysteries
　　to all who peruse our shelves
Take out a book
　　And "play" it!

"one more kiss upon his cheek"

I REGRET

· ·

That one more word we did not speak,
    one more kiss upon his cheek.
One more glance when we departed
    that the whole thing ever started!

"but a hug is so easy to manage"

A HUG

· ·

Packages from the store
    are really a terrible chore.
They're never easy to carry
    and very much contrary.
An umbrella is very perplexing
    on the bus it can be vexing;
And when it begins to rain
    you've left it on the train!
But a hug is so easy to manage,
    no matter how large or small.
It's not heavy like a package
    and one size always fits all!

"a cool date he is"

THE MAN-IN-THE-MOON

I have a date with the Man-In-The-Moon.
     A cool date he is.
I don't really have to dress
     and I can be early or late.
He's never rude and even though
     he's millions of miles away,
His moonlight surrounds my every move.
     A cool date he is!

THE FLY AND THE
BROKEN WHEEL BAR

. . . .

On a hot summer day in a time gone by—
    to escape the stifling heat—
We strolled in this Bar, my friend and I
    and took ourselves a seat.
We looked around at the tired faces
    (and there were quite a few.)
Mostly workers lookin' for places
    to drink a beer or two.
We noticed a lady with a curly wig
    who had been drinking many an hour;
Life for her was boring, you dig?
    So she dissolved into her Whiskey Sour.
Out of the corner of my eye
    I noticed a fly,
who landed on the bartender's nose
    (and boy did thinks get blurry).
He skirted and dodged the bartender's blows
    then dove for the wig in a hurry.
The Lady wanted him out of her hair—
    she didn't like this at all.

continued....☞

THE FLY AND THE BROKEN WHEEL BAR

· ·

She tossed the fly so high in the air
    he bounced against the wall.
The bartender smiled with such satisfaction
    'cause the old fly bit the dust.
So pleased the bug was out of action
    he wiped the wall with disgust.
But, no one saw the falling glass,
    nor the fly move toward the drink.
No one saw the fly (alas)
    more alive than you would think.
Then the pool table bellowed
    with a terrible roar
    and the balls spilled out all over the floor.
The fly buzzed around just one more time
    and headed for the door…
The balls flew after in one long line,
    oh! How the players swore!
We too flew from the Broken Wheel Bar.
    But what I've written is true
And all I can say whoever you are
    May it never happen to you!

*"hands magically connected
to the rock"*

THE PLAYROUND LEGEND

· ·

The face is strong, dark, intent;
 eyebrows knitted down.
Hands magically connected to the rock,
 he moves down the court.
The Ball moves from his hand and back again—
 like a yo-yo:
The Rock flies…flies…
 It glides through the air, high, but true
as if in slow motion, suspended in time
 to its destination:
SWOOSH!
 It falls through the net—almost
 without a sound.
ALL EYES GLUED ON HIM.
 And why not?
Life is basketball;
 basketball is life and
he's a playground legend.

"she is dancing, her hips swaying violently"

THE DANCER OF TOA BAJA

Torrents of rain pound the earth,
　fronds of the coconut palm
　sway in the wet winds.
She is dancing...
　She is dancing...her hips are
　swaying violently,
Her shoulders undulating...
　Pum pum pum pum pum pum . . .
The hands of the drummers escape
　their bodies as they play,
Faster and faster!
　But can you hear the voices;
(The voices in the drums);
　voices of the Island peoples
　who danced here
Like she, so long long ago;
　Free and full of heart, strength and gladness,
They want her to remember their generosity
　Of another time.
She dances, dances, dances!
　Her face glistens and her feet
Decorated with tiny bells, pound the earth!
　The rain pours down and drenches her.
Yes! She remembers you,
　Island peoples of long ago!

"it's working when you should be sleeping"

THE SWING SHIFT

No, it's not a dress or car part,
    and has nothing to do with music.
It's working when you should be sleeping
    and sleeping when you should be working.
Like riding on a Ferris wheel…
    (once a merry-go-round);
But now a frustrated
    roller-coaster.

"just five cents a glass"

For The Young At Heart

THE LEMONADE KIDS

· ·

We were just kids with
    our homemade lemonade stand.
Yelling "Five Cents a glass!"
      "Just five cents a glass…step right up!"
The lemonade was good,
    tasty and cold.
It was our very first 'business',
    we were fearless and bold!
We were the Lemonade Kids,
    skinny and oh so confident
with scruffy brown shoes…
     "Sir? Madam? Just five cents a glass!"

"they stand proud and true"

PALM TREES

· ·

We should be like palm trees;
    they stand proud and true and
    look towards heaven.

They persevere through
    ferocious winds.

They offer food without commitment.

We should be like palm trees.

"he called out for his mother"

TYRE NICHOLS

He was two minutes
    away from his home.
He called out for his mother
    but she could not hear him.

He was brutally beaten and
    died of his wounds.

In our hearts and souls
    we died too.

"and knocked me to the street"

"JUNE 12, 1991"

. . . .

On June 12, 1991 I went out
for coffee on 42nd Street—
   it was not an ordinary break.

Waiting for the light to turn—
   coffee cup in hand;
Suddenly an 18-wheeler delivering Pepsi
   backed into me
   and knocked me to the street!

I scrambled to safety,
   picked up my shoes
   and walked away with
   just bruises on my knees, thinking:

"SUPERMAN, where were you??"

(Song) To be sung along with Plena Music (folk music originating from Ponce, Puerto Rico and environs.)

DRUMS ON MY CEILING

. . . .

CHORUS

I got drums they're on my ceiling
I got drums they're on my floor
I got drums they're in my bedroom
Funny thing is….I want more!

I have a drum—a Conga drum—
    my friends you must be wise:
When congueros touch the cueros
    spirits come alive!

I have a drum—my bongo drum
    I practice it is true;
But you should see my ugly knees
    they're all black-and-blue!

I have a drum a BOMBA drum—
    I play it everyday!
There's a theory drummers say
    that Bomba came from MAYAQUEZ!

continued…. ☛

DRUMS ON MY CEILING

· ·

I have a drum-- a Palo drum,
    for this I wouldn't trade:
Its sound is far and deep and free
    and d'ya know from what it's made?
From an avocado tree!

I have a drum it tells the news
    and anything else you care to choose.
My pandero has many fans
    I hold one [right here!] in my hands!!

So my friends I'm fairly certain,
    fairly certain I will see
another drum tomorrow, another drum for me!!!

CHORUS
I got drums they're on my ceiling
I got drums they're on my floor
I got drums they're in my bedroom
Funny thing is....I want more!

"and slice into a smile"

WATERMELONS II

· ·

Watermelons are green and pink
and slice into a smile.
As I eat and lick my cheek
summer lingers awhile!

"we have movies, music, crafts and moxie"

LIBRARY RAP (EVERYONE CLAP)

Fed up? Listen up! I got a rap for you!
It's not the best but I know it's true.

Whenever you're feeling sad and down,
there's a real cool place
in your own special town.

D.J.'s spin music but we spin much more.
Visit the Library? So you say "What for?"

You can learn anything here—
learn how to cook or weave your hair.

You can take a trip to any place but
keep your shoes on--just in case!

Another great thing about this spot
in the heat of summer it's never hot.

We have movies, music, crafts and moxy
and the people who come here are really foxy!

You can be smart or play the fool—
the Library rocks—it's mad, mad cool.

So tell all your friends and family:
the books, DVDs and internet are FREE!

The Library is fly and has a great rep. . .
the magic begins with your very first step!

PS-- Have you been to the library lately?

"Happy postcards—all were sent."

SUMMER

· ·

Summer's gone used and spent.

Beach balls and picnics are fleeing felons.

Happy postcards—all were sent.

No longer thrive the watermelons.

"He lays his hands on the cueros and begins to play..."

For José Mangual 3rd and in memory of
José Mangual Sr. (Buyú)

EL BONGOSERO

. . . .

With a flourish and a signal the Band begins.

El Bongosero approaches his drum
and places it between his knees.
He lays his hands on the cueros and begins to play:
His hands move across the drum—
how they fly!!

With speed, precision and grace
he caresses and cajoles the drum
as he follows the irresistible melody.

His Solo begins…..
he bows his head for a brief moment:
A furious explosion of rhythms erupts!
The syncopated notes swirl into the air and
surround the riveted listeners…
who leave their seats and begin to dance.

The drum is his life.
His life is the drum!

" *Mom always said since I was two,*
consider practical things to do!."

PAUL GAUGUIN

· ·

If there ever was banality
   it's surely practicality.

Mom always said since I was two
   consider "practical things to do!"

Peter Pan knew from the start,
   the danger of a practical heart;

Always a kid –HE didn't worry
   while WE grew up in such a hurry!

Then there is old Adam and Eve
   who could have argued for a reprieve.

But in the art of being tactical
   they certainly weren't practical!

For Paul Gauguin life was a chore;
   the colors of Paris were a terrible bore.

He sadly departed from family and friends
   and promised someday to make amends.

He discovered islands where color had no limit,
   with Flora and Fauna he became intimate.

With trembling hands he opened a door...
   then he painted a world never seen before!

"the kind that sends them to the cross."

A CERTAIN RELIGION

· ·

There's a certain religion
    that a capitalist loves;

The kind that makes workers
    into turtle doves—

The kind that sends them to the cross
    instead of a meeting with the boss.

The kind that distracts them
    from issues and such

And teaches them never
    to expect too much.

The kind where faith will keep them high
    cuz their apple pie is in the sky!.

A Book of Poetry

TRY YOUR LUCK AT SARATOGA OR DO YOU KNOW WHERE YOUR HORSE WAS LAST NIGHT?

Try as you may, try as you might
  the horse you'll play got drunk last night…

So how to know what a Horse will sow?
  and where he goes when the lights are low?

A Race Horse is not an ordinary steed;
  he doesn't just sit around and read!

He trots down to the old watering hole
  and has a few drinks to calm his soul.

For sure this horse is feeling blue—
  if you had his life wouldn't you?

He remembers when he was running free,
  grazing in the grass of the wide prairie:

The wind in his mane and the warmth of the sun,
  the magnificent moon when the day is done.

Now his life is nothin' but a track
  with some skinny jockey clinging to his back.

continued….

TRY YOUR LUCK AT SARATOGA OR DO YOU KNOW WHERE YOUR HORSE WAS LAST NIGHT?

He might as well trot around a circus rink
    (it's enough to drive a horse to drink!)

And if a horse is drunk, he runs half-hearted,
    which is how this poem got started…

SO, if Saratoga is your next location
    and you decide to make a donation,

Get in line for a bet or two and remember this
    poem and message too:

It's just as plain as a Horse's mane, a pony will
    drink to dull the pain.

And as our horse steps up to the gate,
    sober is what this racing horse ain't!

Saratoga brings the owners big bucks,
    but to an honest horse
    IT JUST PLAIN SUCKS!

All About Fireflies

What makes a firefly a firefly?

Fireflies are a kind of insect. All insects have three things in common: three body segments (head, thorax, and abdomen), six legs, and a skeleton on the outside (an exoskeleton) made out of hard plates called chitin. The name firefly is tricky, because fireflies are actually a kind of beetle. Of all animals, insects are the most abundant; of all insects, beetles are the most abundant. You can find them everywhere except the poles, and you can tell them by their elytra. All beetles have two pairs of wings – a soft pair for flying, and a hard pair – the elytra – for protection.

Where do fireflies live?

Fireflies like tall grasses and standing water; they live everywhere it's wet and warm. There are 2000 different species of fireflies on Earth. A species is a type of living organism, whether plant or animal, fungus or bacteria. When it comes to fireflies, you can tell species (and sexes) apart by the patterns they flash.

How do fireflies live?

Fireflies, like many other (holometabolous) bugs, go through four life stages. In summer, we see adults glowing and flying around. Depending on the species, some adults eat nectar or pollen, some eat other insects, and some even eat other species of firefly! Adult fireflies only live a few weeks – just long enough to mate and lay their eggs in the ground. During fall, firefly eggs remain underground. After a few weeks the eggs hatch into larvae. Firefly larvae live beneath the earth, hibernating through winter and spending early spring eating worms and the larvae of other bugs. In late spring, larvae turn into pupae, which hatch into adults in summer, continuing the cycle.

How do fireflies light up?

Animals that light up, like fireflies, are called bioluminescent. Fireflies bioluminesce with two different chemicals. These chemicals are called luciferin and luciferase, and they work like a lock and key. Luciferase unlocks luciferin, letting in oxygen. Oxygen then combines with luciferin to make light! Unlike a light bulb, firefly light is cold light – the energy it produces is 100% light, 0% heat.

Why do fireflies light up?

Fireflies light up to attract mates of the opposite sex. Males and females of different species flash unique patterns to let potential partners know they're available and interested in mating. But this kind of signaling can be dangerous...

What's the catch?

Lighting up is a great way to get yourself noticed by other animals who want to eat you. However, lighting up can also scare predators away. Fireflies are full of lucibufagins, toxic chemicals which sicken animals that make the mistake of ingesting them. For predators that have suffered this nasty reaction, just seeing a firefly light up is enough to convince them to try another food for dinner. Fireflies also use something called reflex bleeding, voluntarily leaking blood drops full of these smelly lucibufagins, in order to ward off predators. But what happens when the predator is another firefly?

Most of the time, male and female fireflies flash, meet, and mate. But sometimes, the male gets eaten! The female fireflies of one species, Photuris, mimic the flashing signals of females of another species, Photinus. The Photinus male approaches, thinking he's going to get to mate, but when he gets too close the Photuris female eats him! When it comes to firefly love, you never know what you're gonna get.

Are fireflies in trouble?

Recently, scientists have noticed that firefly numbers are declining. Human development and pesticide use can damage their habitats, and light pollution interferes with their mating signals. To prevent the threat to these fascinating creatures, Boston's Museum of Science has started Firefly Watch. At https://www.mos.org/firefly-watch/, you can register as a citizen scientist, helping track firefly populations by observing these insects in your own backyard.

Courtesy of Zachary Velcoff
Cornell University's Outreach Program

ACKNOWLEDGMENTS

THANK YOU!

To my family and friends,
especially my brother Louis and
sister-in-law Roseanne
for
their encouragement and support,
and to all the
world's wonderful poets!

OTHER BOOKS FROM QUIET CREEK PUBLISHING

PAPERBACK JOURNALS

Movie Time Madness

For movie lovers

My Journal

For book lovers

Classic Television Madness

For television enthusiasts

The Music Journal

For music lovers

MEMOIRS

HISTORY

Millie! A Love Story

A true story about unconditional love

Millie! The Last Chapters

The full story from the beginning

AMERICA!

368 pages of early American history

Don't forget to leave a review! Every review matters, and it matters a lot!

To leave a review or for more information on these books, visit www.quietcreekpublishing.com

Jacqueline Andrea Lavalle

Jacqueline has been writing poetry most of her life, but until now never considered publishing. Her poetry has been written over the course of many years, primarily for the enjoyment of friends and family.

Ms. Lavalle received a Bachelor's degree from Hunter College of the City University of New York. She has also earned a Masters of Library Science from Queens College (of the same university) and worked as a Librarian at The New York Public Library and Queens Public Library.

While in Cleveland she was an industrial electrician in the maintenance department at the Jones & Laughlin Steel Mill, establishing herself as the first female to work there since World War II.

Jacqueline has also spent time in Puerto Rico teaching English and is currently studying Afro-Cuban and Puerto Rican percussion. She resides in Flushing, New York.

This is Ms. Lavalle's first book.